20.68

5

PET OWNER'S GUIDE TO THE
AFRICAN GREY PARROT

Annette De Saulles

RINGPRESS

ABOUT THE AUTHOR

Annette De Saulles is a writer and editor with a particular interest in bird and animal welfare, care of the environment and natural healing methods.
Also by the author: *All About Your Parrot*, published by Ringpress Books.

Photography: Keith Allison and Amanda Bulbeck

Published by Ringpress Books,
Vincent Lane, Dorking, Surrey,
RH4 3YX, England.

First published 2000
© Interpet Publishing. All rights reserved

ISBN 1 86054 132 1

Printed and bound in Hong Kong through Printworks International Ltd.

CONTENTS

1 Introducing The African Grey

African Grey parrots *(Psittacus erithacus)* have been kept as pets for centuries, ever since early seafaring days when they were brought back home by sailors. Now, at the beginning of the new millennium, they are more popular than ever – why is this?

One reason, of course, is their unmatched ability to mimic – with uncanny accuracy – human speech, laughter, a ringing telephone, and just about any other sound they hear.

Another, and perhaps a more important reason for its popularity, is the African Grey's capacity to give and receive affection. Like many other species of parrot, a Grey bought as a hand-reared youngster will usually bond with its keeper for life and provide true friendship.

PERSONALITY

In many ways, having an African Grey in the home is like having a toddler who never grows up. Greys are always on the go and like to be into everything. They may scream for attention when you are trying to make yourself heard on the 'phone, or throw a temper tantrum when something does not go their way. They are bright, loving, messy, jealous, noisy and emotional creatures. Besides needing a variety of outlets for their energy and self-expression, Greys also need plenty of sleep – at least ten hours each night.

The African Grey is very intelligent and more highly-strung than some of the other parrot species. These birds notice and absorb everything that is going on around them in the household and will enjoy being included as much as possible in family life. It is very often the case that a male Grey will prefer a female family member, while a hen Grey will

favour the husband or son. Some individuals like to be handled, although others can be quite aloof. However, Greys can bond so closely with their keeper that they become jealous of the keeper's human partner or other members of the family. Establishing what is acceptable behaviour, and enforcing this consistently, will curb any aggression and prevent the situation getting out of hand. Because these birds need a firm and confident approach, they are not suitable as pets for young children.

SIXTH SENSE

The intelligence and sensitivity of the African Grey can be astonishing. A friend of mine, Pete, who runs a small hotel, has a young African Grey called Buffy. This bird had only been with Pete for a couple of months, but was tame, quiet and friendly. He was housed in a large cage in the lounge/dining area, so that he could see everyone who came in and out.

One day, a guest, a perfectly ordinary looking man, walked into the lounge, having booked into the hotel for the night. As soon as he appeared, Buffy went berserk, throwing himself around the cage, screaming and throwing out his food onto the floor. Pete could not understand it as this had never happened before, and he assured the guest that it was completely out of character.

Next morning, when the man came down to breakfast, Buffy did exactly the same thing, kicking up a tremendous fuss and throwing his food out through the cage bars.

It was only later, when the 'guest' informed Pete that he was, in fact, an inspector who had come to check out standards at the hotel, that the reason for Buffy's behaviour became clear. It seems this young Grey had sensed at once that this man was not the ordinary hotel guest he pretended to be!

RELAXING IN THE FAMILY

As your pet Grey gets used to its new family and environment, it will relax and start to whistle, talk and sing. This is where the fun starts, as you rush to answer a telephone that is not ringing or go to let out your whining dog, only to find him fast asleep in his bed. African Greys are clever enough to address family members and pets by name and come out with words and phrases at appropriate times – such as, "See you later" just as you walk out of the door!

By handling your African Grey every day, talking to it, sharing (healthy) human food treats and teaching it to play, you will soon have a confident, chatty and entertaining pet and a valued and important member of the family in its own right.

REFLECTING THE WILD LIFE

Through knowing something of the natural habitat and life of the African Grey, you will have a valuable insight into its particular needs. This is essential in order to provide the best care for your bird in captivity.

Home for African Greys is equatorial Africa, where they live in large flocks in forest and woodland. They enjoy constant

Intelligent and perceptive, the African Grey has an uncanny 'sixth sense'.

fetched for a pet bird kept in a sitting room. But much can be done to provide your Grey with a happy and stimulating life. Companionship is provided by the human family and/or other birds. Healthy, balanced, organic parrot diets are now readily available. Supervised freedom in the home or a garden aviary will give your Grey the opportunity to fly. Toys and games will keep it occupied. Exposure to gentle rain in a garden aviary and/or regular spraying or bathing will keep feathers in good condition.

THE PET BIRD TRADE

Before aviculture became established in recent decades, parrots were acquired by trapping and nest-robbing. This continues today, although, thankfully, there is a growing awareness of the cruelty involved and some governments now outlaw the export or import of wild birds.

companionship within their social groups. Their basic diet in the wild consists of palm nuts, seeds and fruits. Greys need to be able to fly to search for food and nesting places and to escape predators. This provides exercise and occupation. In their natural habitat they are exposed to sun, wind and rain.

You are probably now thinking that all this sounds a bit far-

Being snatched from the wild is traumatic for any parrot and for the sensitive, intelligent African Grey it is disastrous. Many wild-caught Greys never become tame and so are left confined to their cages. Fear and loneliness can then turn them into chronic biters or feather-pluckers – with the

The Congo Grey has spectacular red tail feathers.

result that they are passed from home to home by disillusioned owners.

So, for your own and your bird's sake, only buy a captive-bred, hand-reared bird.

THE SPECIES

There are three distinct species of Grey:

1 Congo Grey *(Psittacus erithacus erithacus)*

This is the largest of the species and the most commonly kept in captivity. It is about 13 inches in length, the male usually being slightly bigger than the female and with a squarer head. The female tends to have lighter grey underparts and a thinner neck than the male. However, DNA or

The Timneh Grey has darker plumage and a maroon tail.

surgical sexing will confirm whether you have a male or female.

The overall grey plumage of the Congo African Grey is dramatically highlighted by its bright scarlet tail feathers and the bare, white skin around the eye. The beak is black, the feet grey. Young birds can be identified by their dark grey eyes, the colour changing to yellow by about two years old.

2 Timneh Grey *(Psittacus erithacus timneh)*
Slightly smaller than the Congo and with darker grey plumage, the Timneh's tail is a dull maroon red. The upper mandible is tan coloured, with a black tip. Timnehs tend to be more laid-back than their bigger cousins and make equally good pets and talkers.

3 Ghana Grey *(Psittacus erithacus princeps)*
You may only realise you have this sub-species by comparing it with a Congo Grey. Ghana Greys are an inch or two smaller and are usually darker grey in colour. Otherwise they are very similar to *P.e. erithacus*.

AFRICAN GREYS AS PETS
Greys can make wonderful, affectionate and entertaining pets. However, before you commit yourself to one of these unique creatures, it is worth considering the following:

With training and supervision, the African Grey will relate to all members of the family.

• Greys can live to about 50 years of age. Provision needs to be made for suitable re-homing should your parrot outlive you!

• They are highly intelligent, sociable birds and therefore need company, attention and stimulation.

• Like all parrots, they can be messy, noisy and destructive.

• Veterinary treatment may sometimes be needed. Specialist avian vets are few and far between – and bills can be expensive.

• Greys need careful and consistent training and handling if they are to remain manageable, well-balanced pets.

Still determined to keep an African Grey? If you are ready and able to meet that list of needs, then you are well on the way to a mutually rewarding relationship.

2 Choosing Your African Grey

Having decided you want an African Grey, you will probably be tempted to rush out and buy the first one you see in your local pet shop. Please think twice. Impulse buys *can* sometimes be successful, but very often they end in disappointment. The best time to buy a Grey is during the summer, when breeding stocks are coming onto the market.

DO YOUR HOMEWORK

Take time to do a little research. Ask at your local Parrot Society branch, if there is one, about reputable breeders. Alternatively, your veterinary surgeon may be able to advise you on this. Make an appointment to visit a recommended breeder and see how his or her birds are kept and reared.

If you are planning to buy from a pet shop or other parrot retailer, go along and make your own checks first:

• Do the birds look lively, healthy and well cared for?
• Are the shop assistants knowledgeable about the birds they are selling and willing to give advice?
• Is any after-sales support offered?

THE PRICE

In the UK, a hand-reared baby Grey may cost £600 or more, so, for this reason alone, it makes sense to take care when buying. If an African Grey is being offered for sale at a price substantially below this, then beware! It may well be a wild-caught individual and, at best, only semi-tame. These birds rarely make good pets.

Do not buy a bird at auction. This is where many wild, sick or stolen birds are sold on. You will not know what you are buying and your 'bargain' may end up being a costly mistake.

15

The best bet is to buy a captive-bred, hand-reared bird. These chicks are eight weeks old, but they will not be ready to leave home until they are at least 14 weeks.

THE BEST CHOICE

The ideal pet African Grey is one that has been captive-bred, carefully hand-reared and which has no fear of humans. Wild-caught, imported parrots will have been traumatised by their capture and journey from Africa and may also be carrying a serious disease which does not become apparent until later.

BABY GREYS

If you are buying a hand-reared baby, the breeder will be able to keep you informed of its progress until it is fully weaned (about fourteen weeks old) and ready to come home with you. It is important that the baby is feeding itself before it leaves the breeder; do not accept a bird that is offered together with a supply of hand-rearing mixture. Good breeders will give advice on caring for your bird and will offer a back-up service in case of any future queries or problems.

OLDER BIRDS

Find out what you can about the history of an adult Grey and why it is being offered for sale. Make sure it is tame and ask to handle it out of its cage. Take things slowly and gently with a new bird, which may bite out of fear. A frightened Grey will growl when approached.

If it is not being sold with an avian vet's health certificate, it would be a good idea to organise this yourself.

Ask about the bird's habits; you will be able to see if it is a feather-plucker, but you may not discover until too late that it hates men or is a 'sunflower seed junkie' – more on that later. It is important to know whether the bird definitely prefers men or women, as a mismatch could mean that your Grey never bonds with you but becomes devoted to another member of the family instead.

Greys will usually quickly make up their minds whether they like you or not, so go by the bird's behaviour towards you when you first meet – this will be a good indication of how your future relationship will turn out. If you are offended by swearing, ask about the bird's vocabulary before you commit yourself.

RESCUE GREYS

There are always African Greys in need of a good, permanent home, although finding a suitable new owner is not always an easy task. These birds have usually been neglected in the past, perhaps over many years, or they may have been handed in to a rescue home when their beloved owner died. Taking on and caring for a rescue Grey brings its own rewards as a bewildered, unhappy bird gradually regains its confidence and health. However, this process can take a lot of time, patience and insight, not to mention the possibility of costly vet bills, and is probably best undertaken by an experienced bird keeper.

LEG BANDS

Responsible breeders will fit a closed ring to the baby parrot's

Details of hatching will be found on the leg band.

Buy the largest cage you can afford.

PROOF OF PURCHASE

Whatever bird you finally decide to buy, ask for a detailed receipt from the seller. This should include confirmation of the species, age and sex (if known) of the parrot and the price you have paid. If the bird is being sold as captive-bred and hand-reared, this should be stated, together with confirmation, if applicable, of an accompanying health certificate from an avian veterinary surgeon.

HEALTH CHECK

A healthy African Grey will be lively, alert and responsive. It will have clear, bright eyes and sleek plumage. Do not buy a bird displaying any of the following symptoms:
• Discharge from the eyes or nostrils.
• Wheezing or laboured breathing.
• A lethargic or fluffed-up appearance.
• Lack of weight or a protruding breastbone.
• Messy vent feathers.
• Watery droppings.

leg. This will give proof that the bird has been captive-bred and will, usually, also give the date of hatching. The latest alternative to this is a tiny microchip implant which can be scanned for its identifying number.

TRUST YOUR INSTINCTS!

Many parrot keepers say that their bird chose them! Do not ignore

It is important to provide a variety of perches.

your intuition – and if the Grey that has caught your attention keeps coming up to the cage bars and looking you straight in the eye, it could just be the right one for you.

ESSENTIAL EQUIPMENT

CAGES
Even if you intend giving your Grey lots of freedom in the home, a good-sized cage is essential for those times when you are not around to supervise.

Invest in a good-quality metal cage with plenty of room for the parrot to stretch its wings and move about freely. Wooden cages are unsuitable as they would not withstand your Grey's beak for long! Plain stainless steel is ideal but, if the metal is painted, make sure the paint is lead-free and safe for birds. The bars need to be sufficiently closely spaced to

Attach feeding bowls to the side of the cage.

prevent the parrot getting its head stuck between them.

There are many cage designs to choose from these days. A cage on wheels is convenient, as it can be easily moved about or taken out of doors when the weather is fine. An opening top, with a raised perch or playstand, allows for freedom while, at the same time, encouraging your parrot to play on top of its cage. This will give it a safe base and also (hopefully!) confine most of the mess and droppings to the cage floor.

Slide-out trays make for easy cleaning and some cages come fitted with an anti-scatter base to catch seed husks etc.

Newspaper makes an ideal cage-bottom lining. It is non-toxic to birds and can be easily removed and replaced each day. You will also probably find that your Grey enjoys tearing it up or hiding underneath it!

Some parrots appreciate the addition of a nesting box to which they can retreat from time to time.

Finally, make sure the cage you buy can be properly fastened shut. Greys do not miss a trick and are extremely adept at undoing any but the most secure catches.

PERCHES

Fit the cage with natural wood perches of varying thicknesses, from three-quarters of an inch to about one-and-a-half inches, and at different heights. These will need to be replaced at regular intervals as your Grey chews through them. However, natural perches will keep beak and feet in good condition, as well as giving your bird an enjoyable occupation. Fruit woods are safest, so it is worth keeping in with a friendly neighbour who has apple or pear trees if you do not have any of your own. Always wash branches carefully before use as they may be contaminated by wild birds or pesticides.

FEEDING BOWLS

Situate one of the cage perches at a comfortable height beside the feeding bowls. These should be of a generous size and made of stainless steel, so that they can be easily and thoroughly cleaned. They will also need to be firmly attached to the cage sides or your Grey will unhook them and throw out the contents in no time! Three bowls are ideal – one for dry foods, one for fruit and veg and one for drinking-water. If you have taken on a very nervous or biting Grey, a revolving 'swing' feeder will allow you to remove and refill bowls without having to put a hand inside the cage.

TOYS

There has never been a wider range of parrot toys on the market and you will soon discover your own bird's particular favourites. The intelligent African Grey needs a variety of toys to keep it happy and stimulated. To shut any parrot away in its cage with nothing to do is cruel and Greys will resort to chronic feather-plucking in this situation.

Buy strong, purpose-made toys from natural materials such as wood, leather and rope. Provide some that are indestructible – for instance those made of acrylic – plus others that can be safely chewed and demolished. Beware of potential hazards such as rings and clips that could trap a beak or foot and do not give your bird ribbon or cord that could get tangled around the neck or wings.

Hemp rope swings will be greatly enjoyed and will also provide exercise for these naturally acrobatic creatures.

Of course, some simple household items make excellent toys. Greys enjoy ripping up the cardboard tubes from kitchen towels or loo rolls and playing with squeaky pet toys. Chewing wood is a favourite occupation, so any safe, wooden items will be destroyed with relish.

Changing toys regularly will prevent boredom. However, take care if you have an older or nervous bird; some Greys will treat any new item in their cage,

TOYS

There is a wide variety of parrot toys to choose from.

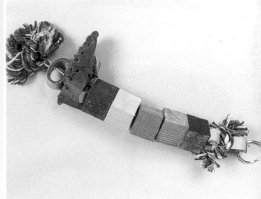

whether it be a replacement perch or unfamiliar toy, with suspicion and fear. If this is the case, take things very slowly and you will gradually build up your pet's confidence and trust.

Incidentally, do not overdo it. Too many toys in the cage and your parrot will not be able to move!

A playstand is an invaluable item of equipment.

PLAYSTANDS

Parrot stands and playframes are a great idea for pet birds and they can now be purchased in a wide variety of designs and sizes. Alternatively, you can make your own. This can just be a simple arrangement, or a more sophisticated combination of natural wood branches at different levels, feeding bowls, swings, ladders and toys. A tray at the base catches droppings and spilt food.

Playstands are ideal for a change of environment when your parrot is out of his cage. Some people take their parrot outside on its stand when the weather is fine. However, it should be remembered that even with clipped wings, a bird can fly a considerable distance if suddenly startled.

OUTDOOR AVIARIES

A simple garden aviary is an ideal way to give your pet Grey exercise, fresh air and sunlight on fine days. Ensure the aviary is cat-proof and that part of the enclosure is covered, to allow shelter from rain or strong sun. You can equip it with a variety of branches, logs and rope swings.

If you are planning to keep more than one African Grey and,

An outdoor aviary gives the opportunity for fresh air and exercise.

perhaps, breed from your birds in the future, you may prefer to house them permanently in an outdoor aviary. In this case, there are several factors which should be considered:

• Are the birds you are buying used to outdoor life or have they been bred for, and previously kept as, house pets?
• Do the birds get on? If you are planning to breed from them, have they been surgically or DNA-tested for gender?
• Would noise from your birds be a potential problem with the neighbours?
• Parrots kept in an aviary will bond with each other, rather than the keeper, and will therefore be less of a 'pet'.

Choose an aviary site that will be sheltered from extremes of weather and provide your birds with as much space as possible. The aviary will need to be of sufficiently strong construction to withstand a Grey's powerful beak. Small-gauge wire will prevent escape and also stop wild birds entering. The base should be concrete and rodent-proof, to prevent the spread of disease from mice or rats. Fully enclosed accommodation will provide shelter at night and in cold weather. In addition, part of the flight should be covered, so that your birds can comfortably perch

Strong, secure aviary construction is essential to keep your birds safe.

there in very hot or wet weather. If the weather turns unusually cold, you may need to consider bringing the birds indoors.

OTHER EQUIPMENT

It is a good idea to have the following items to hand:

- A first-aid box – ask your vet about stocking this.
- A hospital cage or heat lamp in case of illness.
- A sturdy plastic pet carrier for those times when you need to transport your Grey to the vet's surgery, or to its temporary home while you are on holiday. Purpose-made parrot carriers are fitted with a perch and beak-proof mesh front.
- A cheap plant mister for 'shower time'. Alternatively, any wide, shallow bowl will serve as a bath if your Grey will use it (many will not!).
- A length of one-inch dowelling. This is ideal as a training perch if your Grey is reluctant to step on to your hand at first.

• Nail-clippers and a file. Once you are confident about cutting your Grey's toenails, this will save stressful visits to the vet.

• Parrot harness. More and more parrot keepers, especially in the United States, are using a harness to take their parrot with them to the shops or to visit friends. When they are introduced and fitted with care, parrots can quite soon get used to the idea and enjoy being taken out.

It is essential that claws and beak are kept in trim.

3 Caring For Your Grey

Your new pet Grey will need a little time to adjust to its change of environment and human family. If you have a re-homed or a nervous bird, leave it in peace for a while to get used to its new surroundings. Speak to it gently and avoid sudden movements or loud noises around the cage. Even if you intend changing the diet to a healthier one, give your new bird the food it is used to at first and introduce new food items gradually.

A hand-reared baby Grey will adapt much more quickly of course and, indeed, will probably be very demanding of your attention. Resist the temptation to overindulge your baby by letting it have its own way all the time and ruling your life! Lots of handling and cuddles are essential, but so too are routine periods in the day when your Grey is left to play on its own in the cage or on the playstand. By establishing a few firm rules at the start, you are far more likely to end up with a happy, well-adjusted bird, rather than one that bites or screams because it has not learnt where its boundaries are.

SITING THE CAGE

Unless you already have other birds and need to quarantine your Grey in a separate room, it should be housed where there are regular comings and goings within the family – the sitting room being the obvious choice. Parrots are highly sociable creatures and will be miserable left in a room on their own.

A suitable position for the cage is against a wall, away from the television set. Make sure your bird cannot reach wallpaper or curtains, or these will soon be shredded. The cage can be near a window for fresh air and interest, but should not be exposed to draughts, or the heat from direct sunlight or radiators. Always draw the curtains closed at night because night-prowlers such as cats can cause parrots to panic.

The kitchen is not a good place to keep any parrot because of the risk of fumes from heated oil and non-stick cookware.

SAFETY IN THE HOME

Once you have gained your new Grey's trust and it will step on to your hand or a training perch (more on this later in the book), you can let it exercise and play outside the cage.

Always supervise the times your parrot is free. Make sure windows and doors are closed and that other members of the household are aware that your Grey is out of its cage. It is less likely to fly into glass if you take it up to the window, or to a glass door a few times, and demonstrate that this is a solid obstacle. You can also attach stickers on glass as a warning signal. Obviously, no parrot should be flying free in a room with an unguarded, lit fire, and empty fireplaces should be blocked. Do not let your Grey nibble on house plants as some of these are toxic to parrots. Bowls of potpourri may also look tasty, but can be poisonous.

Birds have very sensitive respiratory systems, so never smoke near them and beware of household sprays such as air fresheners and furniture or bathroom sprays. Birds are also highly susceptible to the fumes from paraffin heaters.

The kitchen holds many dangers for parrots, so this should be a no-go area. The fumes from overheated non-stick pans and baking trays can quickly prove fatal and parrots have been known to land on a recently turned-off electric ring which does not appear hot. Electric wires can be chewed through in seconds by a Grey's beak.

Wherever your parrot is flying free, be aware of the possible hazards and remove any potentially unsafe objects that might be flown into or chewed.

A HEALTHY DIET

When living in the wild, Greys eat a varied, seasonal diet of fresh fruits, nuts and seeds, occasionally supplemented by insects and grubs. Your captive bird will depend entirely on you, its keeper, to supply the right foods and it makes sense to follow, as closely as possible, the diet intended by nature.

In the wild, African Greys eat fruit, nuts and seeds, supplemented with insects and grubs.

The importance of calcium

It is worth noting that African Greys can be prone to calcium deficiency which, in protracted cases, may result in permanently weakened bones and beak. It is, therefore, important that this mineral is supplied adequately in the diet. Fresh fruit and vegetables, the occasional small piece of cheese, boiled egg and oyster shell will help ensure your Grey is not calcium deficient.

A seed-only diet may lead to calcium deficiency. The signs of this in a young bird are a soft beak, overgrown joints and stiff, awkward movement. However, this condition can be reversed if treated in time. Your avian vet may prescribe Vitamin D3 or a daily calcium supplement. The provision of grit will help the absorption of calcium and Vitamin D3.

Seeds and pellets

As part of the daily diet, give your Grey a good, complete pellet or seed mix. Buy from a supplier

Make sure the seed mix you buy is fresh and dust-free.

A selection of fruit and vegetables is essential for good health.

with a quick turnover and reject any dusty-looking mixes.

Organic pellet diets are now available, consisting of natural, additive-free ingredients. These pellets look fairly uninteresting compared with the more brightly-coloured complete diets, but they have proved successful in some cases where a parrot would previously only eat seeds. They have also been known to help curb feather-plucking where other treatments have failed.

Fruit and veg

The largest part of your Grey's diet should consist of fresh (preferably organic and seasonal) fruit and vegetables. Feed as wide a variety as possible, as in this way your bird is more likely to get all the vitamins and minerals it needs. Remember to wash fresh produce carefully and clear away uneaten foods each day.

Some Greys will eat anything, others are more fussy, so keep experimenting and encourage your bird to try new things. Apples, oranges, bananas, peaches, nectarines, plums, melon, grapes, pears and strawberries, among other fruits, can be given, as well as soaked, dried fruit for a change. Different vegetables you can try include green beans, cooked potato, carrots, peppers (red, yellow or green), peas in the pod, tomatoes and cucumber.

Regular inclusion of yellow, orange and green fruits and vegetables and egg yolk will guard against Vitamin A deficiency. However, do not overfeed broccoli or spinach, as too much of these vegetables can hinder the uptake of calcium in the body.

Sprouts

For a really healthy addition to the diet, try sprouting your own alfalfa seeds. This can be done in a special sprouter (available in health food shops) or in a screw-top jar, the seeds being rinsed twice a day to keep them fresh while they are growing. As sprouted seeds and pulses can quickly go mouldy, take care to remove uneaten portions regularly and keep feeding bowls spotlessly clean.

Special treats

Cooked pulses, pasta and rice will add variety to the diet and your Grey will enjoy an occasional piece of animal protein, such as a cooked chicken bone with a little meat on it or a small piece of cheese. Parrots also love nuts – walnuts, almonds, natural peanuts in their shell, hazelnuts etc. Do not give your bird too many though, as they are fattening.

Cooked pulses are a favourite.

What your Grey will really love is being allowed to join in with family meal times. The following 'human' foods can safely be fed to your bird as a treat: toast, unsalted crisps (potato chips), plain cake or biscuit, and a chip (french fry) or two – but no salt or vinegar!

A word of warning

Avocado and chocolate have been found to be poisonous to parrots, so avoid these. Salt is also harmful, so do not be tempted to share your bag of salted crisps or peanuts with your Grey – keep a supply of the unsalted varieties for parrot treats.

Nutritional supplements

A varied, balanced diet, high in

fresh fruit and vegetables, should provide all the nutrients needed for good health. However, Greys can be fussy eaters, or refuse anything other than seeds and nuts.

Sunflower seeds are enjoyed by most parrots, but too many of them will lead to obesity and nutritional deficiency. Greys can become 'sunflower seed junkies' if this has been their basic diet in the past. It can then be very difficult to persuade them to eat other things, although it is important to do so. This may take quite a time in some cases, but perseverance is the key. Introduce fresh fruit and vegetables gradually, mixing small pieces in with the familiar diet. If all else fails, provide a vitamin and mineral supplement.

If you think your Grey needs a supplement, consult your avian vet. Extra calcium (see above) or Vitamin A may be needed while you are making the change to a healthier diet. General supplements containing vitamins, minerals and amino acids can be sprinkled on the food, or the soluble variety can be added to the Grey's drinking-water. Mineral blocks are also available and are attached to the side of the cage for the bird to nibble at.

Droppings and empty seed husks collect on the floor of the cage.

A sliding tray makes cage-cleaning quick and easy.

Preening will keep the feathers clean, but a pet bird needs moisture to do this effectively.

CLEANING THE CAGE

A certain amount of mess is inevitable when you keep a pet parrot – droppings, feathers and feather dust, seed husks and discarded pieces of food are an occupational hazard. However, if you get into the routine of cleaning out your Grey's cage every day, this will be a quick and simple job and very little bother.

Make up a solution of hot water and detergent and wipe over the perches before rinsing and drying; your bird is on its feet most of the day, so perch hygiene is important. Next, slide out the base tray and replace the soiled newspaper. Wash food and water dishes thoroughly each day, to avoid the risk of bacterial infection.

Once a week, remove the perches and clean and disinfect the whole cage thoroughly, using one of the purpose-made, safe disinfectants available for bird keepers.

BATHING AND MISTING

African Greys are not known for their love of water, although there are, of course, exceptions to this rule. In any event, all domestically kept parrots need exposure to moisture to keep their feathers in good condition.

Encourage your bird to bathe in a wide, shallow bowl of warm water. Make sure it does not get chilled afterwards and has plenty of time to dry out completely before nightfall. If your Grey does not take kindly to water, get it used to the idea gradually with a brief, gentle misting with warm water from a plant sprayer. Spray upwards over the bird's head, letting the mist fall like light drizzle. In this way your bird may eventually come to enjoy the experience! Remember that the water will feel cooler when it is sprayed, so test the temperature and make sure the mist is pleasantly warm.

Wing-clipping is a controversial subject and bird-keepers need to consider what is best for their own individual parrot.

TOENAILS AND BEAKS

In the wild, your African Grey would be perching and chewing on a variety of branches of varying textures and diameters. In this way, its feet would be exercised and stay in healthy condition and toenails and beak would wear down naturally.

In captivity, parrots need to be provided with similarly varied and uneven natural wood branches. Perches of smooth, round dowelling or, worse still, plastic, mean that the parrot's feet stay in the same position all day and this can lead to physical problems.

Fit irregular, natural fruit-wood perches in the cage, which will exercise feet and help wear down toenails. They will also provide an opportunity for chewing, which will keep the beak in good order and give your parrot something enjoyable to do when it is in its cage.

Keep an eye on the length of your parrot's claws and if they do become too long, your avian vet can clip them for you. Once you have been shown what to do and feel confident, you might want to do this yourself:

If your Grey is nervous, gently wrap it in a towel. Carefully take out one foot at a time. Check to see where the vein ends, then snip off just the very tip of each claw with nail-clippers. Do not cut down too far or the nail will bleed. If in any doubt, just use an emery board instead. If you keep any procedure of this kind as stress-free and brief as possible, your parrot will learn to trust you and get used to it.

If the beak looks overgrown, this should be dealt with by your avian vet. Only the very tip of the upper mandible is trimmed at one time, to avoid bleeding.

WING-CLIPPING

Parrot keepers tend to have strong views on wing-clipping, whether in favour or against the practice. In cases of aggressive, adult Greys, a temporary wing clip is believed by some to be the best solution if the bird is to be brought under control and socialised. Other keepers feel that wing clipping is essential for all pet birds at all times, if they are to be kept safely. However, many have the equally firmly-held belief that parrots were given wings to fly and should be allowed to do just that! Before having your Grey's wings clipped, the following important points should be considered:

• Young parrots need to develop fully physically, and also learn how to fly, manoeuvre, land and balance with confidence before having their wings clipped.

• Do not attempt to clip your Grey's wings unless you are sure about what you are doing. Seek out a reputable bird keeper or avian vet to carry out this procedure. Usually, the trimming of about seven primary flight feathers on each wing will be sufficient to slow a Grey down, without grounding it altogether.

• A badly- or roughly-clipped wing can cause long-term discomfort for the bird and may trigger the habit of feather-picking. A wing which has been cut back too severely – as is sometimes the case with wild-caught birds – may be permanently damaged and the ability to fly impaired.

• Many breeders and retailers advise clipping just one wing, but this can upset a bird's balance and may lead to a fall and, possibly, serious injury. A gentle clip of each wing is preferable.

• Do not forget that even with clipped wings, your Grey will probably still be able to fly a reasonable distance, so do not take any chances. With a tame bird it is easy to become complacent and forget it is perched on your shoulder as you answer a knock at the door or wander out into the garden. All is well until a sudden noise alarms your bird and it flies off. It is also easy to overlook the fact that trimmed feathers do grow back, making your Grey fully-flighted once more.

Most pet parrot owners in the US consider wing-clipping to be standard practice. However, the 'Progressive Wingclip method' has been developed by American aviculturist E.B. Cravens, who writes in favour of natural methods of bird keeping. The progressive wing-clip gently and gradually reduces a parrot's ability to gain excessive height and distance, but without restricting vital flying and manoeuvring skills.

If you prefer to see your Grey flying freely within the home, it is of course important to keep a close watch on it during those times when it is out of the cage. During the warm summer months, windows can be safely left open if a strong frame of suitable wire mesh is securely fixed over them. And if you think your parrot would enjoy coming out with you on excursions, why not try a parrot harness to keep it safe?

If you allow your African Grey freedom within your home, close supervision is essential.

THE ESCAPED BIRD

Accidents can unfortunately happen, and if your Grey flies off, what can you do? First of all, keep calm. Hopefully you will at least have seen in which direction your bird went and it is very often the case that escaped parrots, even if they are fully-flighted, do not travel very far before finding somewhere to perch. It will probably be feeling afraid and confused at finding itself in a new environment and will be sitting quietly in a tree or bush within a few hundred yards of your home.

If you cannot locate your Grey, ask neighbours to look out for it, put leaflets through doors and stick up posters. Ring the police, local animal rescue centres, veterinary surgeries and local radio stations. If there is no immediate news, put an ad in your local paper. Offer a generous reward, in case someone finds your parrot and is thinking of keeping it. Leave the cage, door open, in your garden with food and water inside – parrots have been known to return in this way. Walk all around your neighbourhood, listening. If your Grey does call, you should quickly be able to

Even the most contented bird may make a bid for freedom.

distinguish this from the sounds of other birds.

If and when you locate your bird, the chances are it will be perched high up in a tree – and ignoring your pleas to fly back down to you. This is not because it does not want to, but it will be feeling nervous and disorientated and unsure what to do. Offer a dish of favourite foods and talk to the bird gently and encouragingly – and also be prepared for a long wait!

It may be that your Grey decides to stay in the tree overnight, in which case it is worth going without sleep yourself to keep an eye on it and stay in contact by speaking to it at intervals.

Climbing up the tree or using a ladder might cause panic, but if this seems the only option, approach with extreme caution and take with you a favourite food treat to tempt your bird down. Wear a suitable jumper or jacket in which you can tuck your rescued parrot as you climb down again. With luck and patience, you will eventually have success.

Of course, the way to avoid all this is to always take care with open windows and doors. Also very important is the need to train your parrot so that it steps on to your hand or arm on command and responds to your call. Some owners of Greys have been able to teach their bird to repeat their telephone number or address, just in case they ever get lost!

BEDTIME
Parrots need plenty of sleep, up to twelve hours a night. In the wild, they would go to roost at sunset and wake up at dawn. However, in captivity, the electric lights and television are often still on well

The intelligent African Grey loves learning tricks, and interacting with its human keeper.

If you are going away, you must find an experienced parrot keeper to look after your African Grey.

into the night, which can be stressful and tiring to a pet bird.

Ensure your Grey has plenty of time to sleep and also learn to recognise when it wants to be left alone for a while; parrots need their quiet times, just like we do.

In its natural habitat, the African Grey would not be suddenly plunged into darkness at night, as happens when we turn out the lights. Emulate natural conditions by fitting a dimmer switch, which will reduce the light gradually in the room, like the sun going down.

PLAYTIME
Provided your African Grey is tame, teaching it to play is a great way of interacting and building up the friendship. Being the highly

intelligent creature it is, your Grey will quickly catch on to the idea of fun and games and may even start to think up new ideas of its own!

Greys are ever watchful and will learn a new game by seeing you demonstrate it first. For instance, roll a small ball across the carpet a few times, then let your Grey join in and learn to toss it back to you. (You will find a section on Trick Training later on in this book.)

HOLIDAYS
African Greys usually dislike any change of routine or environment, so if you need to leave yours with someone else when you go on holiday, make sure that person is reliable and knowledgeable about Greys. Friends or relations, if unused to parrots, may not always be the best choice.

You could try advertising locally to make contact with another Grey owner in the same situation, so that you could look after each other's birds at holiday time. Or your bird's breeder may offer boarding facilities. Alternatively, you will find advertisements for

parrot holiday homes in the classified sections of some bird magazines. Always check out the home first and do not be afraid to ask questions before leaving your Grey in the hands of a stranger.

LOOKING TO THE FUTURE
All being well, your Grey is likely to live to the age of about fifty years. It is often the case that a pet bird outlives its keeper and is then offered for sale by relatives unwilling to take it on. This situation is highly stressful to the parrot, which will be missing its beloved human companion and may resort to feather-plucking or biting in its distress. The familiar outcome then is that it is passed from home to home by disillusioned buyers.

Ensure that this does not happen to your own Grey, by making provision for it in your will. It is important to also make sure that the person you would like to look after your parrot in the future is in fact willing and able to do so. If there is no friend or family member agreeable, contact a parrot rescue home who should be able to advise.

4 *Taming, Training And Talking*

aming is important, not only for a happy relationship between bird and keeper, but also because there will be times when you need to catch your bird easily, for instance if it looks ill or has injured itself.

For any kind of training to be successful, your wise and watchful African Grey needs to know that it can trust you, that you are its friend, but also the one in charge of the situation at all times. Put in the time to build up a mutually trusting friendship and give your bird the security of knowing you are the boss. It will then enjoy being with you and will respond far more readily to its training sessions.

Handle your bird every day. Do not wear gloves as this will frighten it, but be patient in encouraging it to step on to your hand by gently pushing your hand against its chest. Teach your bird to take food from your fingers, so

that you will be able to give a peanut or sunflower seed as a reward for progress. Choose a time when your Grey is alert and attentive and keep training sessions short and fun. They should be undertaken by one person only.

NERVOUSNESS

When you bring your new Grey home, it is bound to be nervous of its new surroundings. Put the cage where there is plenty of activity and where the bird can get used to the family, but do not rush into trying to handle your pet right away. In time, it should be relaxed enough to come out of its cage. Just leave the cage door open and let the bird proceed at its own pace. Speak to it often as you pass, in a calm and reassuring voice. Eventually, if you do not make the first move, your Grey will. Take no notice – which is a difficult thing to do – the first time it flies

The new arrival needs to become accustomed to its cage.

Tactful handling is required to encourage the bird to hop on to a perch.

Mission accomplished!

to you or steps on to your hand. If you get excited and make a fuss, this will only scare your bird away! Just act as if you could not care less, which will give reassurance and encouragement. If you are confident around your Grey, this will make it confident in return.

If you have re-homed a Grey that was seldom handled by its previous owners, or have taken on a wild-caught bird, it will be highly suspicious of you and its new environment. This is hardly surprising and you will need to proceed very slowly and gently. However, even a really scared bird can be tamed, so do not give up.

A frightened Grey will often growl when its cage is approached and may panic and flap about, or bite if the keeper puts a hand in to remove it. Some keepers become increasingly reluctant to let their Grey out of the cage because, once free, it flies about wildly and cannot be recaptured. If this is the case, a gentle wing clip may be a good temporary solution, which will allow you to begin taming your bird.

For nervous Greys, US parrot psychologist Liz Wilson recommends taking cage and bird to a small, unfamiliar room, such as the bathroom, having first removed food and water dishes from the cage. Once in this neutral territory, remove the base tray and very slowly and carefully turn the cage upside down on the floor. Make sure there are no objects in the room the bird could hurt itself on if it becomes panicky. Sit quietly and ignore your Grey, who will eventually emerge, although you need to be prepared for a long wait if necessary! This process may have to be repeated quite a few times, but the idea is for the bird to come to you in its own good time. Do nothing to make it lose the small amounts of trust it is building up.

When the Grey is out of the cage and you have then removed the cage from the room, you will be the only familiar thing left for your bird in that room, so it will look on you as security. This is the best time to start the process of taming. As always, do not rush things; act on your own instincts as to how your bird is feeling, and your Grey will slowly learn to trust you.

Once your bird is used to being out of its cage, start training on a carpeted floor, encouraging the Grey to step up on to a stick at floor level by gently pushing the stick against its chest. Remember that it is easier for a parrot to step up rather than step down, so position the stick accordingly. When it has mastered this first stage, gradually get it used to staying perched on the stick while you raise it. The next stage is to get your bird to step from the stick on to its playstand or cage top and then onto your hand or arm. Repeat this training until stepping on to your hand becomes automatic.

Always encourage every sign of progress with praise or a food treat. Many African Greys do not enjoy being cuddled as much as some other species do (for example, cockatoos), but will welcome a stroke and tickle on the back of the head.

When your African Grey is ready to venture out of his cage, you need to establish control so you can move him when required.

Use a perch to tempt your bird to move.

Making the move – a food reward will help your parrot to learn more quickly.

Calm handling will give your bird confidence.

Even tame, well-adjusted African Greys dislike change and are happiest in a familiar routine and environment. Some become panic-stricken when suddenly confronted with a new toy or perch. Others may be afraid of dusters or vacuum cleaners or a particular colour. When introducing new items into your Grey's environment, for instance a new piece of furniture, do this in careful stages and watch for signs of nervousness. Reassure your bird that the object is harmless. If its final position is to be in close proximity to the cage, move the object a little nearer each day. This will usually pacify a nervous bird, but some individuals have been known to pull out their feathers from anxiety, in which case the feared object should be taken out of the room altogether.

If you are planning to re-house the bird in a new cage, do not attempt to make the changeover without first leaving the new cage near the old one for a few days, so that your Grey can get used to it. This also applies to new perches, toys etc. if your bird is afraid of change.

TRICK TRAINING

Your Grey has become a true and trusting friend who has learnt to step up on to your hand or go back into its cage at a word from you. It will now be looking for fun and fresh stimulation – so what better time to start teaching it a few tricks?

African Greys are clever and can learn tricks quite easily. Give your bird a reason to want to do the trick you have in mind. Having your attention is a good incentive, and praise and food treats will encourage it further. Rewards should be given immediately your bird does what you want it to, or it will not know what it is being rewarded for.

Always keep training periods short and fun – no more than about ten minutes twice a day. End on a high note and stop before your Grey gets bored. Use a consistent word of praise, or a small food treat, to let your bird know when it is doing the right thing. Be prepared to be very patient, especially at first, and never get angry with your Grey or punish it. The quickest way to success is to make sure your parrot enjoys what it is doing. If one trick

The tame African Grey will be only too happy to hitch a ride with his owner. However, be aware of the danger to your face or eyes from a parrot's beak.

BEST FRIENDS

*With careful supervision, the African Grey can
be integrated with other pets in the family.*

does not seem to be making any impression, try another, which the bird might prefer: each individual has its own special talents.

Successful US parrot trainer Steve Martin stresses the importance of giving positive reinforcement, rather than negative. That is, give your parrot every reason for liking you and wanting to be with you, rather than making it do what you want simply out of fear of the consequences if it does not obey. Steve advises breaking down a trick into steps and training one step at a time:

• You can teach your Grey to kiss by holding a seed in your lips and directing the bird towards it. Reward and praise your bird for being in the right position.

• If you want to teach your Grey to wave, put out your hand as if asking the bird to step up. Reward it for lifting its foot – but before it touches your hand. Repeat the action, giving a reward this time when the bird lifts its foot a little higher than before. After a time, it will have learnt to wave. If you wave your free hand at the same time that your bird waves its foot, it will learn to respond in this way in the future.

• You can teach your bird to pick up an object by first rewarding it for touching the object, then for picking it up, then for holding on to it for a longer period of time.

There are many other tricks that can be taught, depending on your own Grey's character and preferences. Some Greys, especially if taught to do so as babies, will lie on their backs and can be taught to roll over and 'play dead'. Gradually limit the rewards to encourage your bird to lie still for longer periods. Shaking hands can be taught by gently shaking your Grey's foot with one finger and saying, "How do you do?". Your clever bird will soon learn to put the action and words together.

Remember to use consistent words or phrases for teaching each trick and think up tricks that will use those actions that come most naturally to your bird.

Getting the desired results may take a while, but just be patient and keep persevering.

A final word on trick training: do not be disappointed if yours is the kind of Grey unwilling to perform tricks. While being perfectly capable of doing them, some individuals simply choose not to!

SPEECH TRAINING

If you want a parrot that talks, sings, whistles and imitates just about any other sound it hears, the African Grey has to be right at the top of the list. Although there are some individuals who never get round to saying much, the majority of Greys, once started, are difficult to stop.

You will probably be able to teach your young Grey to whistle before it starts talking, as whistling is a natural call for it. Before it actually starts talking, it will be listening to everything going on around it, so be careful what you say if you do not want certain words or phrases repeated later on! African Greys can start talking at just a few months old, but some do not say much before they are about a year old. After this time, their vocabulary usually increases quite dramatically.

Keepers of these clever mimics will tell you they have rushed to answer the phone time after time, only to find it was their Grey doing a perfect imitation of the ringing sound. It will order the pet dog to 'sit' or 'be quiet', and the poor confused animal will immediately obey. The ping of your microwave timer will mysteriously go off ahead of time

and you will hear your husband or daughter talking in the sitting room, only to find there is no-one there but your Grey having a cosy chat all by itself.

These clever birds not only mimic the sounds they hear, but learn their associated meanings. If you always yawn towards bedtime and then occasionally also say, "Time for bed", your Grey will begin saying "Time for bed" just because it has heard you yawn. Some relations who were looking after a friend's Grey told off their children at dinner time for making such a scraping, clattering noise as they ate. Then they realised it was the parrot doing a perfect imitation of knives and forks on plates. It had already learned to associate this noise with mealtimes, so would start making these sounds as soon as the family sat down to eat.

If you are anxious for your Grey to learn to talk, but feel you do not have the time to train it, you can buy pre-recorded speech tapes and CDs which can be left to play periodically in your absence, or the keeper can record whatever words, phrases or songs he wants the parrot to learn. However, your Grey would much rather have you there in person talking to it, so

Teach your parrot to wave.

With practice, you can achieve synchronised waving!

Acrobatics are no problem.

The party piece!

recorded speech without the addition of personal interaction is probably not the best option. Also, hearing the same word or expression repeated over and over again gets boring after a time, so your Grey may just ignore it, or get in the habit of talking only when it is on its own! In any event, it will almost certainly learn to talk without the need for CDs, tapes, radio or television – or even any particular effort from you.

If your Grey seems reluctant to start talking, it may just need a bit of encouragement from you. Do your speech training in a quiet room, so that your bird is not distracted by other noises. Wait for those times when you are both relaxed and your bird is looking attentive. Speak to it in a really animated voice, repeating a few times the word or phrase you want it to learn. Do this at regular intervals, but never for long periods, as Greys have only a limited attention span. You can also repeat the words being taught as you pass the cage at other times of the day. Praise success and your bird will soon have a wide repertoire of words, expressions,

songs, whistles and many other sounds. Just remember that patience is the key.

POTTY TRAINING

The drawback to giving your Grey freedom in the house is finding droppings deposited on the furniture, carpet – and yourself. But the good news is that you can train your bird to eliminate in a place of your choosing such as the playstand, for example, where droppings will fall on to the newspaper in the tray below and can be easily cleared away.

Study your Grey's body language and learn to recognise when it is about to eliminate. Hold its tail gently upwards to delay the action and place your bird on its playstand, saying "OK", "Paper" or whatever word you have chosen for this purpose. If and when you get a satisfactory result, give lots of praise and perhaps a small food treat.

If you continue with this training, your bird will quite soon learn to associate the command with going to the loo and, in time, will automatically return to its playstand for this purpose.

5 Behavioural Problems

T he African Grey's exceptional level of sensitivity and awareness means that it can also be prone to behavioural problems in captivity. However, many of these problems can be minimised, or avoided altogether, if the keeper establishes the ground rules for desired behaviour right from the start. It is important to be consistent. Ignore bad behaviour – parrots hate being ignored – and give positive reinforcement when your Grey does what you want it to do.

A Grey that is given inconsistent or conflicting messages from its keeper will be confused and insecure, and this can lead to a bird that is out of control.

WHO IS IN CHARGE?

In the wild, Greys understand that there is a flock leader. In your home, that flock leader needs to be you. This is the first and vital step to ensuring that your pet Grey understands who is in charge and who it can trust to lead the way. Many behaviour problems, such as screaming and biting, stem from the pet Grey attempting to take charge of the household because the keeper has never made it clear who is boss.

Once the pecking order has been established, your parrot will be able to relax and everyone will have a happier time.

Establish a few simple commands and enforce them every time you want your parrot to obey; it is important that your bird does not feel he has the choice.

To start off with, a bird that is unwilling to step on to a human hand may be prepared to step on to a training perch instead.

Always use the same word and action for whatever you want your bird to do. "Good" and "No" will soon be understood, as will "Up" when you want your Grey to step on to your hand and "Down" when you want it to step down. (US writer Sally Blanchard describes how to establish correct control over a parrot in this way in her 'Nurturing Dominance' method.)

Also remember that your Grey will be in a more submissive position perched on your hand or arm, rather than your shoulder, where it will consider itself your equal.

It may take a while before these commands become second nature to your Grey, but just be patient – it will be time well spent!

SPOILING AND OVER-BONDING
Spoilt Greys are just like spoilt toddlers who throw a tantrum the moment their mother turns her back. If you do not want a parrot like this, resist the temptation to spoil your new baby.

A baby parrot will test everything with its beak, including your fingers, but it is a good idea gently to discourage this behaviour so that it does not develop into full-scale biting later on.

Get your parrot used to the idea that you cannot always be with it and it cannot always be flying free in the room or sharing your TV

dinner! Make the cage a welcoming sanctuary with food items that take time and trouble to eat, such as peas in the pod or pomegranates. Fit hemp ropes and ladders and natural perches to chew.

Establish a routine with your baby Grey and stick to it. In this way, your bird will soon know when it can be with you and playing out of its cage and when you will be absent, or busy doing something else in the room.

If you give your baby Grey all your time and attention at first, this is what it will always expect. African Greys, in particular, react badly when they no longer have the attention they are used to, and the result can be chronic feather-plucking. As always, establish the ground rules and stick to them.

AGGRESSION AND JEALOUSY
We have seen that an African Grey can become aggressive if it is not given clear and consistent rules as to how it should be behaving and if allowed to believe it is head of the human 'flock'.

Aggression can also occur for reasons of jealousy. Because a parrot will usually bond with a particular member of the family – and not always the keeper – it may take an active dislike to the chosen human's spouse. As far as the parrot is concerned, the spouse is a threat to its relationship with its beloved mate. It is common for a hen Grey to prefer the man of the house and vice versa. Jealousy can take the form of biting or dive-bombing the victim and can become a real problem if not curbed.

Make sure from the start that your Grey is used to being handled by several members of the family, so that it does not become fixated on its keeper and aggressive towards anyone it perceives as a rival.

Take care also before introducing a new bird into the household. Your Grey may be jealous of the imposter and attack it. The birds will need to be introduced very gradually and watched closely until you are sure they are getting along.

If you have already taught your Grey the meaning of "No", and to

Do not allow your African Grey to become fixated on one person.

step up on command, you are in a good position to discourage aggressive behaviour before it gets out of hand. Greys are very observant and watch our facial expressions closely. If your bird shows aggression, say "No" very firmly and give it the fiercest possible glare. Then turn your back and walk out of the room for a few minutes. Never hit your parrot, which will destroy its trust in you, or shout at it, which it will enjoy.

ADOLESCENCE AND BREEDING BEHAVIOUR

If your tame and loving young Grey seems to have turned into a Rottweiler overnight, the reason could simply be that it is starting to grow up! As the hormones kick in, your parrot may start to become noisier, or uncharacteristically aggressive. It may also become particularly possessive and amorous towards you, or whoever is its chosen human 'mate'. It is best to discourage this behaviour by gently but firmly removing the bird and distracting its attention elsewhere. When your Grey is out of its cage, watch it closely for aggressive attacks, particularly on its human rival.

Once a Grey is mature, breeding behaviour usually occurs for a few weeks once a year. You may find your bird shredding up the newspaper in its cage in an instinctive attempt at nest-building. It may also regurgitate its food to you, or whoever is its human 'mate', or start displaying more often than usual.

This period will pass, so just relax and sit it out. If your Grey is behaving particularly aggressively, it is safer to leave it in its cage rather than risk being bitten. In any event, do not punish your bird for what is, after all, perfectly natural behaviour.

TURN DOWN THE VOLUME!

African Greys are not generally the noisiest of parrots, especially if captive-bred and carefully hand-reared, although they can learn to imitate other, noisier species if kept with them. It should also be remembered that all parrots need to make themselves heard occasionally, just as they would call to each other in the wild.

If your Grey is over-noisy, it may be that it is simply reacting to the high noise levels around it, from the television, stereo or arguing children, for example. Or it may be frustrated from over-long periods in its cage with

Adolescence can be a testing time.

nothing to do. If you try and see things from your bird's point of view, you may quickly understand what is making it unhappy.

You can encourage your bird to be quiet by being quiet and calm yourself in its company. However, if your Grey is driving you mad with its screeching and you cannot find any obvious reason for it, do not despair. Once you understand a bit of parrot psychology, you can start to remedy the situation.

Many pet parrot keepers, when their bird starts screaming, will naturally want to quieten it down. They get irritated and shout back. Or they take the bird out of its cage and distract it with a tasty treat. All parrots like to get their keeper's attention and they also enjoy a good shouting match and food treats. So you see, by reacting to your Grey's screeching in this way, you are simply encouraging it to make more noise than ever!

Difficult as it may be, the best way to discourage screaming is to ignore it. If you cannot stand the noise, leave the room. Only give your bird your attention again when it is being quiet. In this way, it will learn to associate being quiet with positive feedback, and realise that being noisy will get it nowhere.

BITING

It is not surprising that a bird snatched from the wild will be afraid of humans, and will quickly learn that the only defence it has against humans is to attack with its beak. African Greys are particularly nervous parrots and many wild-caught individuals get passed from home to home because they are 'biters' and their keepers fear going near them.

However, without early and consistent discipline, even a captive-bred Grey, as it starts to mature, may surprise its keeper with a painful bite. If it has never been shown where its boundaries are, it will be testing out the

Nipping is totally unacceptable, and this lesson must be taught from day one.

relationship and attempting to gain control. This, however, is a confusing and insecure situation for the parrot – and a potentially dangerous one for the keeper.

Ensure that your Grey understands right from the start that nipping is unacceptable. It needs to know that you are head of the flock and totally in charge so, if you can manage to keep a straight face – which is difficult – when your bird bites, this will increase its confidence in you. *Never* hit your Grey, as this will only increase the nervousness that probably made it bite in the first place. As with all unwanted behaviour, a firm "No!" accompanied by a fierce look will usually get the message across.

By studying a Grey's body language you will get to know the warning signs that it is likely to bite. However, special care needs to be taken if you have acquired an older bird that can be unpredictable.

FEATHER-PLUCKING

Plucking or chewing the feathers can be one of the most difficult habits to stop, once started. Because they tend to be highly-strung and more easily stressed than some other parrots, African Greys can be particularly prone to it.

If a Grey starts to pluck out its feathers, it is usually for one or more of the following reasons:

- Frustration and loneliness from confinement in the cage for long periods.
- Lack of mental and physical stimulation from toys, natural wood branches etc.
- Lack of opportunity to exercise/fly.
- Confusion as to its place in the family – or 'flock'.
- Stress from a poor or polluted environment.
- Haphazard routine; insufficient peace and quiet to rest.
- Coming into breeding condition.
- Change of family circumstances or environment.
- Distress at the keeper's absence.
- Attention-seeking.
- Poor diet, high in fatty foods such as sunflower seeds and peanuts.
- Incorrect wing clipping.
- Central heating/lack of opportunity to bathe.
- Overlong periods of darkness/light.
- Parasites or liver disorder.

If your Grey is plucking its feathers, it is a good idea first to take it to your avian vet for a thorough health check. Once any physical cause has been discounted, you can then reassess its diet and living environment. In the majority of cases, this habit is directly related to life in captivity, rather than to any physical problem.

Have there been any major changes within the home – someone moving out or in, a new baby or pet, maybe just some new furniture in the parrot's room? This can be stressful enough to start your bird pulling out its feathers.

Is the bird left in its cage all day while you are out at work? If so, is there any way in which you can rearrange your routine at home so that your Grey has company and

Feather plucking may be an attention-seeking device.

can be out of its cage for longer periods?

Does it have enough to do? Provide occupation, interest and challenge with a playstand, new toys, ropes, wood to chew on and items to destroy. Give food that takes a while to eat; make a small crack in the shell of a walnut to start it off and your Grey will enjoy the challenge of opening the nut and picking out the contents. Take the time to play with your bird, teach it tricks, get it accustomed to regular warm baths or misting.

If you suspect the plucking is a way of getting your attention, try ignoring the behaviour and then making a big fuss of your bird the instant it stops it. As mentioned before, parrots love the excitement of being yelled at, so telling your bird off for feather-plucking will only make the situation worse.

Can a favoured family member or friend look after your bird in its own home while you are away? Or can you take your bird on holiday with you?

If your Grey is hooked on sunflower seeds, chop up raw fruit and veg into tiny pieces and mix these in with the seeds. Most of the healthy food will probably be discarded at first, but your Grey will be forced to eat at least very small amounts and hopefully will, in time, get used to the idea. You could also try a vitamin spray on its usual food, which will encourage it to start eating healthier foods and will also supply necessary vitamins in the meantime. It is also thought that organic complete pelleted diets can be helpful in discouraging some feather-pluckers.

An Elizabethan collar may be used in some cases of feather-plucking, but this can be distressing to the parrot, which may well start plucking again as soon as the collar is removed.

Some parrot keepers are turning to holistic remedies for psychological problems such as habitual feather-plucking. Acupuncture, homeopathy and herbal remedies are all worth investigating.

Your avian vet may advise certain drugs to curb the habit, but the first priority is, of course, to recognise the underlying cause of feather-plucking and to make the necessary changes in the Grey's life and environment.

6 Health Care

Y ou will have read earlier in this book about the importance of choosing a carefully weaned, captive-bred parrot and providing it with a varied diet, hygienic conditions and a good environment. These factors will go a long way to ensure that your Grey stays healthy and happy. However, if a parrot becomes ill, it can then deteriorate quickly, so keep an eye open for any change in your bird's appearance or behaviour. Always have the telephone number to hand of a specialist avian vet, in case you need it in an emergency.

If your Grey displays any of the following symptoms, do not hesitate to contact the vet: discharging eyes or nostrils; abnormal droppings; fluffed-up appearance; lethargy; messy under-tail feathers; noisy breathing; loss of appetite; dull or closed eyes; sitting on the floor of the cage; lack of preening.

FIRST AID

At the first signs of illness, call your avian vet and remove your Grey to a warm, quiet place where it has access to food and water. Keeping a bird warm when it is unwell or in shock is vitally important. Place it in a heated hospital cage, or under a heat lamp if you have one, and wrap it in a towel for the car journey to the vet.

It is a good idea to have a first-aid nutrient formula available. These emergency supplements, available from avian healthcare suppliers, can keep a bird alive until it is able to start eating normally again. Alternatively, as an emergency measure, give your Grey a warm glucose solution from a syringe to help replace fluids and to provide energy.

In the case of accidents, try not to panic or you will only add to your bird's fright. Speak to it quietly and use slow, calm movements. Keep styptic powder handy to stem blood flow from a broken claw or blood feather.

Parrots can get caught up or injured when playing with what might have seemed like a harmless toy or ordinary household object. If your Grey has got a foot or wing tangled up in thread or wire, or has got its beak or head trapped in some way, stay very calm and talk reassuringly to your bird as you carefully free it.

If your bird has an injury you cannot easily treat yourself, or you think it has eaten something that might be poisonous, call the vet at once.

COMMON AILMENTS AND TREATMENTS

Sore or swollen feet

Feet can become sore and toenails overgrown if cage perches are inadequate. Smooth, round dowelling or plastic perches are not suitable, long-term, for parrots. Perches should be of natural wood with the bark left on and in a variety of shapes and textures. In this way, your Grey's feet will get the natural exercise they need.

If a leg or foot looks swollen, this might be as a result of an outgrown ring. It is important to have the ring removed as soon as possible by your vet. Do not delay, as it could mean the loss of a foot.

Feather-plucking

Avian vets must see more cases of feather plucking than any other parrot ailment and, unfortunately, this condition seems to be particularly prevalent with African Greys. The problem is that, like the human habit of nail-biting, once started it is difficult to stop.

Your avian vet can check for dietary deficiency, mites and other possible physical causes. A bad wing-clip can lead a parrot to pick at its feathers if the shafts have been damaged and are causing discomfort.

The most common reason for feather-plucking, however, is boredom and distress. It stands to reason that an intelligent creature like the African Grey will be reduced to pulling out its own feathers if left in a cage all day long on its own.

See the advice earlier in this book on curbing this habit with environmental improvement, diet, toys and bathing.

In chronic cases, your vet may prescribe drugs, a restraining collar or beak notching.

Vitamin A/calcium deficiency

This problem occurs in Greys that are in the habit of eating only seeds, so that they refuse all fresh fruit and vegetables. If baby Greys are fed an inadequate diet while they are growing, they may develop rickets. It is therefore essential to establish good eating habits right from the start.

It may take quite a while to persuade your Grey to eat a healthier diet but, in the meantime, a liquid or powdered supplement will help. African Greys in particular need a plentiful supply of calcium in the diet. Symptoms of calcium deficiency may include convulsions and trembling. Providing a piece of cuttlefish is insufficient, but a deficiency can be treated with Vitamin D3; ask your vet for advice. Good foods to give are: a chicken bone with a little meat left on; a small piece of cheese; scrambled egg that includes some of the crushed-up eggshell.

Chronic sinusitis, where the nasal passages become blocked, can result from poor diet, in particular one lacking in vitamin A where sunflower seeds are the main food eaten.

SERIOUS ILLNESSES

The following are some of the more serious diseases and infections that can affect African Greys. However, remember that these are rare in captive-bred birds that are provided with a healthy lifestyle and kept away from other, possibly disease-carrying, birds.

Aspergillosis

This is a fungal infection which affects a parrot's breathing and which can be recognised from the symptoms of weight loss, a change

in the sound of the bird's voice and frequent bouts of exhaustion. It can prove fatal if not caught in time and will spread rapidly in aviaries of stressed, wild-caught birds. Your avian vet can test for this disease.

The fungal spores of aspergillosis thrive in damp, mouldy foods, so always buy your parrot food from a reputable supplier with a quick turnover.

Psittacosis

This bacterial infection, which is fairly common in imported Greys but much less so in captive-bred individuals, may be carried for some time before symptoms appear. Do not buy a bird from an aviary where one of the other birds looks ill. It is a good idea to have your new bird checked out by an avian vet who will be able to test for the disease.

Psittacosis is usually spread when a bird inhales infected faecal dust. Young birds are particularly susceptible to infection from their parents. It can also occasionally be spread to humans, the symptoms being similar to those of a bad case of 'flu. If your bird has been tested positive for psittacosis, you should let your own doctor know that you are at risk.

In parrots, the symptoms can include laboured breathing, coughing, sneezing and nasal or eye discharge, a lack of interest in food, diarrhoea and a depressed appearance.

Antibiotics are used to treat psittacosis in both parrots and humans.

To avoid the risk of your Grey contracting this disease, keep any other newly-purchased bird quarantined before allowing the birds to come into contact with each other. If you have been to a bird show or pet shop where you have been handling other birds, wash your hands carefully before touching your own Grey. Some parrot keepers change their clothes as well in these circumstances, just to be on the safe side.

Polyomavirus

This serious disease, which is shed in the faeces, can be spread from one bird to another without any symptoms becoming apparent until it is too late. However, it is far less likely to occur in a pet parrot that does not come into contact with other birds.

Polyomavirus is most commonly seen in young birds. Some of the warning signs are

lethargy, vomiting, diarrhoea and bleeding beneath the skin. The good news is that a vaccine has been developed at the University of Georgia in the US and this is proving successful in preventing infection in nearly all cases. A responsible bird retailer will be prepared to have young stock vaccinated before selling them on.

Psittacine Beak and Feather Disease

There is as yet no cure for this virus, which can be recognised by a distorted, overgrown beak and severe feather abnormalities and loss. Some parrots can live for some time with PBFD, but will usually succumb to a secondary infection or disease.

7 *Breeding African Greys*

The desire to breed is a natural instinct which we deny a lone pet parrot. Agitation, aggression and nesting behaviour can be seen as Greys come into breeding condition. This seasonal phase will normally pass without too much trouble, with your bird returning to its usual, happy self a few weeks later. However, some individuals will resort to feather plucking from frustration. A hen Grey may lay eggs in her cage and if these are removed by the keeper she will keep laying, with the probable result being calcium deficiency or prolapse.

If this is true of your own Grey, or yours is an imported bird that has never become properly tame, you may decide the best option is to allow it to go into an aviary to breed. This can work well, but there are also some important factors to consider first.

A Grey kept in the home for some time will have become accustomed to human company and the family routine, as well as a warm environment. Suddenly putting it out into an unfamiliar aviary to live with one or more of its own kind can be highly stressful and may trigger an illness. Make the change gradually, acclimatising your bird by putting it in the aviary for short periods at first during warm weather. Greys are quite hardy however, and once used to being outside, your bird should adapt well to its new environment if the aviary is well sheltered.

Always introduce new birds on neutral territory. Use great caution and watch for any sign of aggression. You also need to be aware that, once your Grey has a partner of its own kind, it may become indifferent or aggressive towards you, even if it was tame before.

Ideally, if you are thinking of breeding African Greys, you will already have gained some experience with one or two of the easier psittacine species, such as budgerigars or cockatiels. An understanding of the paired Greys' needs is necessary for success and the following points should be kept in mind before you start.

1. Males and females are monomorphic, that is, they look alike, so to be sure you have one of each, surgical sexing or DNA-testing from a blood or feather sample is necessary.

2. It is not always enough just to put a male and female together in

The male and female African Grey look identical so you may need DNA testing to establish you have a pair.

an aviary and expect them to breed. Some parrots just do not get on, or one or other of the pair may be sexually immature or infertile. Ideally, a pair should be allowed to choose each other from an aviary group. Watch for displaying and mutual feeding as a hopeful sign that you have a compatible male and female.

3. Greys need to be given privacy if they are to breed and raise young successfully.

4. The nest box needs to be to their liking.

5. Although African Greys are not the noisiest of parrots, if you live in a built-up area and are planning to keep your birds outside,

neighbours' complaints need to be considered.

6. Even if you are intending to let the parents rear their young, you will need to be prepared to hand-rear the babies if any problems arise in the nest box. This means round-the-clock feeding for the first week.

7. Breeding pairs need extra calcium. Include food items such as scrambled egg (with a little shell), walnuts, sprouted seeds and pulses, sweetcorn and peas with the usual variety of seeds, fruit and vegetables. You can also use a calcium supplement.

8. A hand-reared baby Grey in the UK will fetch in excess of £500 (about US $750). This may sound quite a lot of money, but against this should be set not only the cost of special food for the parents and babies, but the many unsociable hours that need to be put in by the breeder to hand-feed the young.

HOUSING AND NEST BOXES

African Greys can be bred indoors but, ideally, the pair should be given an aviary where there is sufficient room for them to fly about freely, as well as an enclosed shelter for privacy and protection. The flight needs to be covered in

The nest box should be lined with pinewood shavings.

part against wind and rain and must be strongly built to prevent the birds chewing through the woodwork. Supply natural wood perches and wooden toys for your birds to chew on to save the aviary frame.

Nest boxes should be about 12 ins (30 cm) square x 24 ins (60 cm) deep, with extra pieces of wood fitted inside for the hen to chew on and a ladder attached from the entrance hole. Put in a few inches of pinewood shavings for the nesting material.

Fix a choice of nest boxes in secluded corners of the aviary, about six feet up, and be prepared to wait quite a time before your birds start to show any interest. A newly-introduced pair may take many months before they are settled and ready to breed. The birds may simply sleep in the boxes at first.

Once you suspect chicks have been hatched and you want to keep an eye on their progress, wait until the parents are absent before you inspect the box or they may abandon the nest.

Eggs are usually laid in the spring, with an average clutch size of three. The female incubates the eggs for 28 days. During this time the male will feed his mate and continues to do so after the babies have hatched, while also helping her with the feeding of the chicks. The newborn chicks have pink skin and fluffy white down. The grey feathering starts to come through soon afterwards and is complete by nine weeks of age. At about 12 weeks old they are ready to leave the nest and about two weeks later they are beginning to feed themselves. At this stage the eyes are black, this colour changing to yellow in the adult bird.

HAND-REARING

The correct method of hand-rearing parrot chicks requires a degree of knowledge and skill beyond the scope of this book. It is therefore essential to ask for advice and help from a knowledgeable breeder before you undertake this task.

Of course, African Greys themselves will always be the best parents for their young. We humans can only do our best to imitate nature. But if you have decided to hand-rear, the best time to take the chicks from the nest is when they are about 12 days old. Sometimes hand-rearing becomes a necessity in any case, if the parents are not caring adequately for their young.

You can make a brooder from a plastic tub lined with paper towels, or soft cotton fabric, that cannot catch on the chicks' toenails. As the babies get a little older you can use pinewood shavings instead but, whichever lining you use, it will need changing frequently. Make sure the chicks are neither too hot nor too cold. They will look agitated and pink in colour if too hot, huddled and quiet if too cold.

Hand-reared chicks can be best fed from a teaspoon with bent-up sides. They will need feeding every couple of hours at first, the time between feeds reducing as the birds get older. Specifically-balanced hand-rearing foods can be purchased, which provide all the necessary nutrients. Alternatively, you may want to make up your own formula. Seek

At three weeks old, this chick is well practised at taking food from a teaspoon.

advice on this from an established breeder of the species.

Take care, when feeding, that the formula is at the correct temperature and not too hot. The chick's crop has a very obvious bulge when it is full and looks flat when the baby needs feeding.

From about eight weeks of age the young Greys can be gradually introduced to solid foods such as small pieces of fruit, peas and soaked seed. As the birds learn to crack seed and feed themselves, the hand-fed formula meals can be reduced.

It is vital that baby Greys are fully weaned and eating dry foods before they go on to their new homes. The new owner will need full instructions as to their bird's feeding and care, and the offer of a back-up service in case of any difficulty.

With this good start, both African Grey and proud new owner are well on course for a happy life together.

At eight weeks of age, the brood is thriving.

BIOLOGICAL DATA

Name:	African Grey (*Psittacus erithacus*)
Distribution in the wild:	West/Central Africa
Natural diet:	Nuts, fruits and seeds
Life span:	Up to about 50 years
Weight:	Congo: 450 grams
	Ghana: 375 grams
	Timneh: 300 grams
Length:	Congo: 12 inches
	Ghana: 10 inches
	Timneh: 9 inches

Colour: Overall grey – darker in the Timneh and Ghana.
Scarlet tail: Congo and Ghana.
Maroon tail: Timneh.
Bare white areas around eyes, which is yellow in an adult bird, dark grey in a baby. Grey feet.
Black beak: Congo and Ghana.
Horn-coloured beak: Timneh.